ACKNOWLEDGEMENTS

To De'Yana Fowler my granddaughter you inspirer me every day. Your experience of being bullied and overcoming bullying was the fuel for this book. We want to teach others not to remain silent when someone is hurting them. Speak out. This kills the bully spirit. It shows other people who they really are and stops the punishment. Don't suffer in silence. You always have a friend at A.N.T.S. Anti-bullying Not Today Stop. contact us at antsontherise.com. Look out for more Yani books as she gets older and changes lives. I wrote the book for you but you're the owner and creator of this story. I love you and as you grow always remember your grandmother loves you. Keep changing and inspiring the world.
Love Glamma

COPYRIGHT 2020 :COPYRIGHT:
DEMI FOWLER ALL RIGHTS RESERVED .
ISBN 978-1-7353630-0-4

This document is geared towards providing exact and
reliable information in regards to the topic and issue covered.
No part of this book may be reproduced in
any form or by any electronic
or mechanical means including information
storage and retrieval systems, without permission
in writing from the author. The only exception is
by a reviewer, who may quote short excerpts in a review.
The trademarks that are used are without any consent,
and the publication of the trademark is
without permission or backing by the trademark owner.
All trademarks and brands within
this book are for clarifying purposes only
and are owned by the owners themselves,
not affiliated with
this document

YANI CHANGES BULLYING

Demi Fowler
De'yana Fowler

ANTI-BULLIYING NOT TODAY STOP
A.N.T.S.
This book is about kids, but it's based on how strong and resilient ants are to overcome bullying.
We have to become and Ant community working together to take care of each other to stop bullying.

Mom Dad It's the first day of school I'm in Kindergarten. I can't wait to meet all the new kids. I'm going to make lots of friends.

Okay honey, you know our home address right. Yes, I do and you and Dad number by heart. Grandma bought me this new phone too. She told me not to let anyone see it unless I'm in trouble.

What is trouble? Like if I see someone with a gun. I run and then go to the nearest adult and tell them. I call you, dad, or grandma and tell you immediately once I'm safe.

So are you to play with your phone at school.
No! Ma'am, only if something happens
and I can't get help. I call my family.

Do you show the phone to anybody? No, not even my teacher should know I have it.

As they pull up to the school, Yani's mom asks her, Do you have your money for lunch?. Yani smile, yes mom, I'm ready for school.

Yani walks into the class and is in awe of all the kids; they are beautiful. All colors of the rainbow.
Her teacher Mrs. Riley is very nice.
She has a huge smile, and her voice is so soft.
She greets all the kids with hugs.

Yani makes friends with several kids. Sara, Valencia, Russell, Charle Gwen. They share lunch with each other daily. One day while at lunch, a first-grader named Megan threw gum in Yani's hair and started laughing. Yani tried to get the gum out of her hair, but she could not. She told the teacher Mrs. Riley, and she used ice to freeze the gum to get it out of her hair.

Once Yani got in the car with her mom. Her mom would ask daily; how was your day? Yani would always put a smile on and say it was a good day. Then she would tell her mom about P.E. and other class activities. Her mom would ask her what has she done today to help someone else make their day better. Yani would say I gave all my teachers hugs.

So what did you learn today? Not everyone is nice to you. Yani, why would you say that. Just because some kids are not. Well, Yani make sure you stay away from the kids that are not nice okay, baby. Yes, Mommy.

Yani wakes up excited about going back to school the next day. Yesterday was surely an accident. Megan could not have meant to throw gum in her hair. Yani was the only child, so she loved school because she got to play with other kids.

Yani bought an extra snack today. She would give it to Megan. Maybe she just wants to be friends with me, Yani thought. As lunch started Yani got in line. She got her tray of food and walked over to where Megan was.

Megan always sat at the table alone. So, Yani put her tray down next to Megan's apple. Megan never had lunch, just something small daily Yani slid in the seat next to her. Yani held out the snack for Megan to take.

Everyone in the cafeteria was watching the exchange. No one ever sat with Megan because she had hit and took items from most of the children in the cafeteria. They never told anyone what Megan did because they hoped she would stop bullying them, but she had not.

Yani was smiling as she brought out the snack she gave Megan. As soon as Megan saw the Cafeteria worker's leave. She pushed Yani whole lunch onto the floor. She then pushes Yani on to the ground as well.

As Yani cried, she promised herself that she would always avoid Megan. Once Sara and Yani returned to the cafeteria, everyone was lining up to leave lunch. Neither of the girls got to eat lunch that day. After school, Yani's Dad picked her up and asked the same questions that they would ask daily. Yani answered them all with a huge smile on her face. Leaving out the part about Megan.

A couple of weeks had passed. The once happy Yani had started hating going to school. She no longer woke up before her alarm clock. She stayed in bed most mornings even after she's awake. Her mom and dad had noticed the change and asked her daily, but she always had a great day with a story to tell them.

No one but the kids in Yani class knew that Megan was bullying Yani. She had pantsed her on the playground. She had thrown her and her lunch on the ground several times. Even cut a piece of her hair. Yani was very afraid of Megan that she tried everything to make Megan like her, but it didn't work.

When Yani got up, she ran to the restroom. The three women split up as Yani's mom ran after her to the restroom. The principal and her grandmother went over to Megan immediately. The principal also told Megan to come with her to the office.

Meanwhile, back in the restroom, Yani was surprised to see her mom, but she was also very happy. Her mom asked her was she okay. She asked what happened to make her cry. Yani told her mom part of the story. She said she dropped her lunch. Her mom now knew why she was always so hungry after school.

Yani's mom told her. You do know you can always talk to me about any and everything.
If someone is hurting you, don't be afraid to tell me.
Yani started crying again.
She told her mom of each, and every time Megan had hurt her.

Yani's mom explained to Yani that she was being bullied. She told her that being bullied was not her fault. She explaine that bullying is when another person tries to intimidate someone or perceive them as weak. Bullying can be in a lot of different forms, from hitting to doing embarrassing things to someone. Fighting them or even speaking down to them or about them to others.

Yani's mom told her if anyone ever did that to her, she would not get in trouble, but she needed to always tell her family the truth. The other person would not get in trouble either but get help. She explained that usually, a person is a bully for a reason, and we just have to make sure they are okay.

Yani and her mom walked to the principal's office. As they entered, they saw a crying Megan. The principal and Yani's grandmother had spoken with her about the issue they saw, but after Yani's mom told them of the other incident. Megan's parents were called immediately.

Megan and Yani's parents met in the principal's office. After Yani's parents explained what was going on with Megan, her parents could not apologize enough. They also learned that Megan's older brother had been treating Megan the same way she was treating Yani.

Megan's parents went home and spoke with Megan's older brother. He stopped bullying Megan, and Megan also stopped bullying Yani. Bullying creates a harsh cycle. Once the bullying is exposed, it can be stopped. There are ways to make things better for people getting bullied and the bullies. Sometimes all the people involved just need to be heard.

Hurt people hurt people, so if someone is hurting you. Speak out to someone and let someone know. Never suffer in silence. Use your voice. It could help not only you but someone else. You have to become like A.N.T.S. Be stronger than your body weight, help build a strong unbreakable bridge of friends, work hard at being heard. We are going to work diligently AS A COMMUNITY LIKE ANTS to stopping bullying together WE CAN DO IT.

More Info on ants reference

www. antsontherise.com

www. Thoughtco.com

www. pestworldforkids.org

Fun Facts about Ants

1. Ants have super human strength.
2. Soldier ants use their heads to plug holes.
3. Ants form symbiotic relationships with plants.
4. The total biomass of Ants equal the biomass of people.
5. Ants where the first to start farming before humans.

Anti-bullies. Not. Today. Stop.

Lightning Source UK Ltd.
Milton Keynes UK
UKHW050942280820
368833UK00002B/9